LIFT UP THEIR HEARTS

Visiting Older People

Mary Threadgold RSC

Published by Messenger Publications, 2023

ISBN: 9781788126557

Designed by Edel O'Dea
Printed by Peninsula Print

Messenger Publications,
37 Leeson Place, Dublin D02 E5V0, Ireland
www.messenger.ie

Lift up Their Hearts is dedicated to all those people who, either through family commitment or by their own choice, become regular visitors to older people who need them and their company. The following words are addressed to them:

> "I will not wish you riches nor the glow of greatness
> but that wherever you go,
> some weary heart shall gladden at your smile,
> some weary life know sunshine for a while,
> and so your path may be a track of light,
> like angels' footsteps passing through the night."
> Author unknown

Mary Threadgold RSC

 CONTENTS

⊰⊱ INTRODUCTION ⊰⊱

Lift up their Hearts contains some guidelines and is a practical resource written for the benefit of anyone visiting older people in Nursing Homes or visiting those housebound in their own homes on a long-term basis. It is relevant when visiting older people who are mentally alert and are interested in general conversation, including talking about current affairs, the current state of the world and their world.

However, sections are also included for later stages of dementia, for those coming towards the end of life and for those occasions when visiting restrictions are in place, such as in a pandemic. It is meant as a resource rather than a textbook so the visitor can refer to a particular section when needed, hence the likelihood of occasional repetition in the text.

It is written in two parts: Part 1 is for general use, while Part 2 is for those for whom spirituality is particularly valued. While the emphasis will be on Christian denominations, mainly Roman Catholic, it can have relevance to other non-Christian denominations.

When an older person is living on their own or in a nursing home, loneliness and a feeling of loss, especially the loss of independence and familiar company, as well as reduced choices, can be keenly felt. The joy of a visit from a familiar person can mean such a lot to them.

1

Every situation is different. In some cases, conversation comes easily since both parties have a lot in common and have a lot to share. In other cases, ongoing regular visits may prove a challenge.

This booklet is compiled to provide a resource to meet such a challenge. Suggestions and insights will be offered depending on the individual's needs and interests.

Some are happy with an occasional unscheduled visit, but others value a regular visit and a commitment on the part of the visitor.
A scheduled visit means that the individual has something definite to look forward to.

Some of those being visited are particularly drawn to spirituality. Suggestions based on an RC religious background are offered, but it depends on whether the visitor and resident feel comfortable engaging at this deeper level.

Others are living with dementia, and they need an approach that includes an element of routine as well as a sensitivity in conversation. Suggestions are offered to help make a visit fruitful for both parties.

The person being visited and the visitor, whether in a nursing home or at home, whether male or female, will be referred to as 'she' to make for simplicity throughout this booklet.

The bottom line for both resident and visitor is meaningful and enjoyable conversation. If this flows easily, you may not need any of the suggestions given in this booklet. If conversation does not come easily, then I hope that some of the contents of this booklet will be a help.

⇜⇜ PART 1 ⇝⇝
BEFRIENDING

Social Visiting

Some residents prefer a surprise and unscheduled social call with no commitment on either side. This preference is respected and responded to. They may be people who are unwilling (or unable) to explore how they feel emotionally and may avoid talking about themselves apart from selective factual information or reminiscing about what they worked at, where they lived or visited while on holiday or whatever common experience they share with the visitor including hobbies or other areas of interest.

Occasional short visits, scheduled or unscheduled:

This kind of visit can be enjoyed by the person being visited as a surprise which interrupts a very regular schedule. Being visited gives the resident a sense of their value, that they are worth a visit and have been thought of. It helps the resident to feel less lonely. The resident enjoys news updates, even if occasional. If there is no commitment to a particular day or time, greater flexibility is afforded to the visitor.
A disadvantage if unscheduled is, that often the person to be visited is otherwise engaged.

Regular visits, scheduled, more personal visits:

The benefits, in this case, include the fact that the resident can look forward to the visit, knowing that the visitor is reliable and will come. Some residents like visitors to do some helpful chores on a regular basis, or the visitor might bring that person's favourite newspaper, magazine, sweets or other items. The visitor's commitment to visits gives the resident an added sense of their own value.

Companionship Visits

This involves committed visits to older residents in nursing homes or in their own homes in order to give the recipient a feeling of being loved, valued, listened to and understood. Visits are arranged for a day and time that suits the resident, the visitor and the schedule of the particular location. Once this is a regular visit, it is important to communicate this fact to staff looking after the resident.

The visit aims to be meaningful, enjoyable and relevant to each individual being visited. Many residents enjoy conversations based on their interests and preferences. Conversation needs to be life-giving with some degree of depth. Chit-chat and gossip are avoided. Companionship aims to add quality to the visiting experience (being given time to express their own feelings etc.).

Many older people enjoy reminiscing about many aspects of the past (including their life story), learning to live in the present, listening to favourite songs, music or poetry, engaging the senses (taste, touch, smell etc. either separately or as a 'pampering session') or favourite religious practice (Rosary, Psalms, specific prayers, readings, Lectio Divina or other prayers that the resident finds uplifting and is comfortable with). Spiritual reminiscence is about finding meaning in life, gratitude for life's blessings or an opportunity to re-frame painful memories. It is about celebrating and coming to terms with who you are.

The length of visits varies with the preferences of the person being visited, but this could be 15 mins. 30 mins. or 45 minutes. Initially, it would be good to visit weekly, but this could be reduced later to every two weeks. A way needs to be found (either on a calendar or diary) to alert the resident when to expect the next visit. Without this, you may find an empty room when you arrive and will spend an amount of time trying to find the person. It also deprives that person of the enjoyment of anticipation.

It is important that the visit ends on a positive note, with an uplifting thought or insight, an indication of when you will see them again and /or a prayerful conclusion.

The benefits of companionship visits:

A warm and trusting mutual relationship develops. It gives the resident something positive and enjoyable to think about after the visit.
The resident looks forward to a dependable visitor. Mutual trust plays an important part. The visitor respects the importance of the visit to the resident and takes the commitment seriously.

Companionship - Useful Information

1. The qualities of the visitor that enhance the visit:

- The visitor needs to be natural – happy to be herself. It can be easy for the resident to sense if the visitor is genuine and sincere.

- She has a sense of commitment and is dependable.

- She is a person with emotional warmth and an easy smile but is not over-effusive.

- She can relax with others and give herself wholeheartedly to the visit, sitting at an appropriate distance, not too close or too distant from the resident, with an awareness of the resident's ability to hear and understand.

- She can think creatively and imaginatively and put herself in the resident's shoes.

- She understands the need for preparation, thinks ahead before the visit and comes equipped with anything needed that day.

- She remembers to spend a few minutes letting go of personal preoccupations before meeting the resident and focuses her full attention on the visit.

- She needs to be fully present to the resident and take time to listen and engage, giving the impression that she is relaxed and not watching the clock.

2. Communication:

This is a two-way process:
    (a) using speech and language
    (b) listening, and understanding the other speaker
The third dimension of communication is non-verbal, used often unconsciously by both the speaker and the listener. Don't ever forget that you are communicating with the resident through your unconscious facial expression (e.g. a smile, a frown, a look of disquiet or annoyance), through your tone of voice (e.g. kindly and caring, impatient or cross), or through your body language (relaxed or tense, engaged or distant).

In using speech and language, we do so, among other things, to ask questions, give information, express choices and preferences, say how we feel, share our worries, our joys and our ideas, tell stories or jokes, deceive, negotiate etc.

Communication involves a speaker and a listener; this implies turn-taking so that one party does not do all the talking, nor do they interrupt the other. Silence is an integral part of conversation, so the visitor must be comfortable with and allow for periods of silence during the visit.

3. Introduction to the senses (hearing, sight, taste, smell, touch):

Some sensory stimulation could add to the quality of the visit. We have learned from philosophy that there is nothing in the mind that hasn't first been experienced through the senses; therefore, the senses give us access to the brain and sharpen the person's ability to focus attention and concentration. Even a small amount of sensory stimulation (e.g., hand cream/hand massage for smell and touch) can help the resident to be more alert and focused as well as being an enjoyable and relaxing experience for them (provided of course, they would like it).
With regard to <u>taste</u>, make sure that the item given is allowed for medical reasons.

They can use the sense of <u>sight</u> to look at pictures or photographs or whatever items are present within their range of vision, just as their <u>hearing</u> is stimulated by the sound of their visitor's voice.

This aspect of visiting will be expanded on in the section on 'The Senses' p.18

Another important part played by the senses is that in engaging them, you can trigger memories, e.g. the words and melody of a particular song can evoke pleasant or unpleasant memories; the same could be said for memorabilia associated with school days, e.g. a ruler or a copybook or a poetry book or a piece of chalk; smelling mothballs, tasting *Irel Coffee* or feeling a piece of silk or veiling.

4. Practical Issues that you need to be alert to when visiting:

- Has the resident had a recent adverse experience, e.g. the recent death of someone close, has been unwell, had a bad night or a fall?
- Do they have a problem with talking or understanding due to a stroke or other neurological condition?
- Do they have a problem with a hearing aid, denture or glasses?
- Have you checked to see if they have a swallowing problem, in which case the 'taste' item may need to be omitted?

Arranging Visits

Setting up and establishing these visits on a regular basis:

Be definite about the arrangement and initially consider having a typed note to remind the person being visited, e.g.

```
Name (of person to be visited)_____
Your visit with (visitor)_____
will be on_____(day/date) at _____

A visit can last either 15, 30 or 45 minutes
and we can plan together to make it a meaningful and
enjoyable time for both of us.

You can choose how we will spend our time
together, perhaps just in conversation, or
reminiscing about life, listening to our
favourite songs, music or poetry, waking up the
senses and helping with concentration, and giving
us a sense of achievement and fulfilment.
```

Conversation:

Priority is given to conversation so here are some tips. A good starting point for any conversation is to remember the need for a relaxed atmosphere, so:

Relax - Relate - Communicate

This is true for all forms of conversation if it is to be a good experience.

Conversation is also about taking turns as the speaker and as the listener. As the speaker, you can gently introduce new topics from time to time using some of the techniques outlined in the next section. These include reminiscence, music and poetry, engaging the senses etc.

- Be sure to have something to speak about – a knowledge of the other person's interests, your shared history, hobbies etc.
- Make sure you can be heard and understood, and speak at an appropriate pace.
- Do not dominate the conversation.
- Be aware of your non-verbal communication – eye contact, facial expression, tone of voice, and body language.
- Engage at a suitable distance, neither too close nor too far away.

Balance speaking and listening:

- Give the other person your full attention. Cut out distractions, TV etc.
- Watch the other person's non-verbal communication to make sure that you have their attention, eye contact, facial expression, nods, and interested tone of voice.
- Try to give the impression that you have all the time in the world by being as relaxed as possible.
- Do not interrupt.
- Let the person know you are listening by reflecting back what you have heard them say.

So far, under companionship visits, we have looked at ways to engage the person we are visiting with, e.g. conversation, reminiscence and enjoying poetry, songs or music.

We will now look at engaging the senses, knowing that this helps the person to be more alert, with a better ability to focus attention and concentrate, as well as possibly the triggering of memories.

Various examples will now be given of resources that the visitor can gather and have some (or even one example) available when visiting the older person.

Reminiscence and the Resident's Life Story

Introductory facts:

"Memories confirm that each person is unique and individual. Thinking and talking about one's past life can help reduce feelings of loneliness and isolation" *(from 'A pocket book of memories' by Shepherd and Rusted).*

Reminiscence is about reliving in the present and in some detail, something experienced or felt in the past. Personal memories are a means to an end so that the individual feels a resultant increase in self-esteem, companionship and enjoyment.

A Life Story takes a holistic view of the span of a person's life and the different phases that have made up that life. It will include how they felt about events and experiences as they were growing up and reaching adulthood. It can include significant relationships and their attitudes to school and education in the broader sense. It can take in their interests, hobbies and travels.

For many older people, standing back and looking at life objectively can be of great benefit in changing their perspective and hopefully giving them insight into events and relationships that shaped their lives positively or challenged them in some way. The support of an understanding and compassionate listener can help integrate adverse experiences when viewed after the passage of time.

Memories are often triggered by reminders such as photographs, songs or various paraphernalia such as an old fountain pen, a headscarf or brooch.

Reminiscence resources:

Reminiscence is no more than a conversation using the past as the primary focus. To begin with, choose and explore a topic and bring it alive together. Memories can be triggered at any of the following levels at which they lived their lives.

Physical triggers: can include the environment in which they lived, their home, its furnishings, their neighbourhood or parish, country, and past travels. Further examples include what they wore, the shops they remember, the food they ate, games and sports they played or listened to on the radio or a description of a favourite place.

Social triggers: include family, friends, playmates, schoolmates, doctors, nurses, clergy/religious, or local church, people they admired, singers, film stars, clubs, social groups, music they loved – name it, who sang it, what they associate with it.

Intellectual triggers: can include their memory of school, college, teachers, lecturers, books they read, writers, artists, hobbies, performances they attended, special interests and skills.

Emotional triggers: are a very important part of reminiscence, so they remember how they felt about life events, relationships, and experiences - happy, sad, angry, and grateful. It gives them an opportunity to reframe and adjust their thinking about life experiences.

Spiritual triggers: You will find that everybody can recall significant moments in their lives which continue to hold very deep meaning for them. Such triggers can include memorable days, celebrations, uplifting experiences, deeper aspirations, prayer, retreats, faith friends, interest in the arts, music, poetry, natural beauty or whatever made life meaningful for them.

Be tentative initially when using these triggers and remain alert to the feelings and emotions being evoked – be very careful to let the resident set the parameters for every conversation and never probe more deeply than they are clearly willing to go. Your prompts and responses should be invitational and straightforward, never forceful or pressing.

NOTE: *Not all the resources mentioned in this booklet will suit every individual being visited. The visitor needs to know each person's likes and dislikes. Ask their views on this and where necessary, speak to another appropriate person.*

The following two sections about music, songs and poetry, and sensory stimulation will expand on ways of valuing and including these in the visit. They are meant as a resource rather than a programme and would need some level of preparation on the part of the visitor.

Enjoying Poetry, Songs and Music

66

Poetry is language in service of the unsayable.

Poetry:

Poetry has the capacity to tap into the human spirit; good poetry is akin to spirituality. Poetry learned in one's youth is often easy to recall and can trigger memories, both of words and associations.
Some individuals prefer to listen to poetry being read aloud or recited well rather than reading it themselves. This also applies to other readings, e.g. Shakespeare or classical passages, e.g. 'There is a time for everything....'

According to the philosopher Heidegger, 'Poetry is language in service of the unsayable', so good poetry can open up great meaning and be a gateway to a person's deepest hopes and fears. It can be a portal to our spirituality.

Ways to enjoy Poetry:

- Access old poetry books e.g. 'Favourite Poems we Learned at School' or 'Treasury of Poetry'.
- Identify personal favourites e.g. 'Daffodils', 'The Lake Isle of Innisfree', 'The Brook' or 'All in the April Evening'.
- Read familiar poetry aloud and with feeling for the person being visited.
- Build up a collection of quotes from Shakespeare or other passages previously studied at school and share these with that person.

Apart from poetry, some older people might like the visitor to read a book with them or even to borrow a library book for them.

❝ *Music taps into the human spirit.*

Songs and Music:

Music/Songs resonate because of the beauty they embody or because they are particularly meaningful to the listener.
Music/Songs reflect different moods (they can either stimulate or suggest tranquillity or nostalgia and lift the human spirit).
Music/Songs facilitate companionship (choirs, singalongs, music sessions, marching bands).

Ways to enjoy songs:

- Find out if the person being visited has favourite songs or hymns that they like to sing.
- A selection of these songs can be compiled to make a playlist (see Sally Magnusson – 'Playlist for Life' to learn more about devising a personal playlist).
- Singalongs from the second World War can be popular, e.g. 'Pack up Your Troubles' and 'Keep on Smiling'.
- It is said that songs we sang between the ages of 15 and 25 years are most easily recalled.
- Many enjoy listening to the singers they remember from their youth, e.g. Bing Crosby, Doris Day, Burl Ives, John McCormack, Joe Dolan or the Clancys.
- Religious songs/hymns, especially if they can join in the chorus. e.g. 'Bring Flowers of the Rarest', 'Hail Glorious St.Patrick.'

Ways to enjoy music:

- Play music to suit the person's mood – quiet lullabies or stimulating pieces with a good beat, evocative music, meditative, easy-listening and nostalgic music.

- Rhythmic music can be accompanied by an instrument such as a drum or castanet.
- March music/Souza, dance music/Strauss, céilí music such as the Kilfenora Céilí Band or Scottish music can easily be accessed on YouTube.
- Classical Music – play the person's favourite composer, musician or selection of orchestral music. Since 1991 when the Mozart effect was explored, it is generally agreed that there is insufficient evidence for the original claims of benefits. Still, classical music, in general, may enhance some brain functions. YouTube's online video-sharing platform, which can be accessed on a smartphone or tablet, has abundant choices available.

Card Games or Board Games:

Some residents may have a particular interest in card or board games. Discuss this with them or family members to see if they would like to have these games available to them or bring one along if a family member suggests it and see how they respond to it.

Engaging the Senses

In this section, we look at more examples of how you might introduce sensory materials during your visit.

(a) Taste:
(always refer to nursing staff for clearance of items to swallow.)
Sweet tastes: mint, various fruit juices, ground almonds, cloves, sherry, treacle
Savoury flavours: Bovril, mustard, vinegar, ginger, pickles, horseradish

If appropriate to the situation, bring small cheese biscuits and make miniature snacks – soft cheese, ham, fish paste, dates, marmite, crisps, grapes - cut in two - along with a drink to wash it down (coffee, fruit juice or personal choice, even if that is water).

(b) Touch:
(Make sure to follow up-to-date infection control regulations regarding proximity and touch.)
Physical touch: handshake, gentle massage on shoulders, holding the person's hand
Tactile: rummage bag of textures or small items, e.g. seashells, acorns, jewellery, small bottles; handling small items (possibly taken from shelves around the person's room)

Hand massage: (with or without hand cream)
(*If using hand cream, check first that it is suitable for use with the resident; if in a nursing home, check with the nursing staff.*)

- Sit beside or in front of the person, whichever is most comfortable.
- Put a small amount of hand cream on the back of one of the person's hands.
- Stroke the back of the person's hand from wrist to fingertips - 15 times.
- Stroke the front.
- Use your index and middle fingers on top and your thumb underneath and gently pinch each finger + thumb from base to tip.
- Do this on each hand.
- Use just enough hand cream so as not to leave hands wet or sticky; otherwise, use a hand towel to dry off excess hand cream.

(c) Smell

Visitor could bring one (or some) of the following items with her when visiting:
- Perfume or aftershave
- Spices, cinnamon, coffee, cloves
- Mothballs/camphor
- Lavender oil
- Lily of the valley
- Hand cream
- Shoe polish + nail polish remover
- Dettol, TCP
- Citrus zest
- Eucalyptus
- Carbolic/Coal Tar soap

(d) Hearing

- The Human Voice in greeting and conversation
- Music – on YouTube, e.g. Jimmy Shand; Mise Eire, including the option of a small drum to beat along with or a tambourine
- Songs – personal choice, songs to join in with (singalongs)
- Poetry - Poems from school days to join in with, favourite poets old and new (e.g. Pam Ayres, Seamus Heaney etc.) Listen to a poem being read (e.g.Patrick Kavanagh, Brendan Kennelly)

(e) Sight

- The most welcome sight of seeing the visitor
- Visitor wearing something distinctive, a colourful scarf, a piece of jewellery or cross
- Pictures, photographs, memorabilia, including objects from around the room
- Books or pictures of young children at play and having fun
- Books of flowers, gardens, nature, views/scenery – all natural beauty
- Books of young animals at play, puppies, kittens, lambs etc.

Visiting a person living with later stage dementia

For many people living with dementia, the guidelines and resources given in the 'Companionship' section of this booklet will provide adequate options to fall back on if needed. However, in the later stages of dementia, when conversation can be a problem, other approaches may be necessary. This section is specifically for those visiting a person living with more advanced dementia, where the two most important things to remember are:

- The demeanour of the visitor – loving and respectful
- Some measure of routine to foster familiarity and anticipation on the part of the person being visited.

This visit should take place in a quiet, undisturbed environment for the purpose of focusing attention and helping the person to stay socially connected to the visitor and the world around them. They can often make eye contact and smile responsively, indicating a form of non-verbal communication (facial expression, body language, tone of voice). They can be very sensitive to the visitor's tone of voice, which needs to be caring and patient. They need reassurance and affirmation and a feeling of being loved and valued.

Many will respond to familiar materials when presented to them. Their long-term memories can be triggered and shown, for example, in their ability to join in old familiar songs, hymns or poems.
It would be helpful if the visitor were to wear something familiar that is easily recognised, such as a scarf or other item of clothing; a piece of jewellery such as a cross or other pendant; a distinctive perfume or aftershave, to trigger recognition of the visitor by the resident.

The natural qualities of the visitor are important, such as:
- Emotional warmth with an easy smile but not overly effusive.
- Attentive listening (shown by nods, facial expressions and body posture) and waiting without jumping in and interrupting.
- A relaxed demeanour, pausing and allowing sufficient time for the other to respond.
- Flexibility; can balance the need for routine while being open to appropriate alternatives.
- Being committed and dependable, arriving on time,
- Being well prepared, noting the resident's interests and preferences and bringing along items that make for an enjoyable and interesting visit.

As a visitor, you will need a level of self-awareness:
- Be yourself; when you are natural, the person you are visiting will sense this, and it will help them to be at ease with you; the visit will be meaningful to both of you.
- A meaningful visit will take time, including time to get to know the person you are visiting. What you learn will give you insights to help with future visits.

Sample Routines as Resources for the Visits:

This routine will take approximately 30 minutes. If this is too long, keep to the pattern but omit some of the items, with the intention of building it back up again when this is appropriate. Remember that engaging the person you are visiting through easy conversation is the most important of all. Their need to connect with others is of prime importance; the other items in the routine are tools to help them do this.

Arrival:

Make your knock at the door, and your greeting become a familiar one. Wear something familiar like a scarf, a brooch, a cap or a hat.

- Then identify yourself: The visitor can begin by confirming the name of the person being visited, "Your name is" (or "you are" or just say the name of the resident) "My name is....."
- "You are from", "I am from...."
- "You were (occupation)", "I was (occupation)"

These are just samples; it might be appropriate to say something about family or a particular hobby or interest.

Conversation:

Go over relevant news or happenings, and remember **NOT** to ask questions and **NOT** to argue but to listen and watch for indications of the individual's feelings during this interaction and respond to these.

Sense of Touch/smell:

If it is appropriate to do so, offer hand cream and a hand massage (see under 'Companionship')
As an alternative, have several small items with you in a bag for the person you are visiting to see, feel, and identify.

Familiar verses:
Have a few poems that this person knows (e.g. Innisfree, Trees), music on YouTube (Jimmy Shand), Prayers or hymns (have names of family members on a card to be prayed for)

Reminiscence:
Tourist postcards of Ireland to talk about; family photographs if available; build up memories by talking to family/friends, e.g. travels and other experiences, and have these written down to trigger memories.
Many older people love looking at pictures of happy children, even if not their own.

Sense of taste:
If it is appropriate and in keeping with medical advice, give one 'After Eight' or a piece of fudge.

Finish up:
Talk about your next visit. If the person is religious and RC, bless with Holy Water.

An Alternative Type of Visit (if eating /drinking is allowed)

1. *Arrival-* familiar knock on the door or other greeting on arrival
2. *Conversation-* as appropriate, e.g. about visitors who came since the last time
3. *Snack-* bring snack items with you, and having checked the appropriateness of the item with staff or family, let the resident see you making it up with cheese biscuits, cream cheese or Easy Singles, cooked ham, grapes or dates cut in half lengthwise, crisps and any other small items that would be suitable, such as a soft drink. Take plenty of time to prepare these to be consumed in a leisurely way. This will engage all the senses as they see and hear what you are doing, taste and smell, and feel the texture of the items as they eat them.
4. *Wash Up-* the resident listens and, if possible, watches as you do this.
5. *Phone calls-* if they would like and can identify whatever friend you put on and can interact with them for a short time.
6. *TV-* if they like television and you know the programmes they used to watch, use the zapper to move along the channels, stopping for a while with one they enjoy.
7. *Music jingles-* associated with programmes they enjoyed in the past,e.g. The Riordans, Glenroe, O Donnell Abu, Hospitals Requests, etc.
8. *If religious-* have names of family and friends on a card or have their photographs and pray for each one and say something about them that they might recall. Include familiar texts, e.g. "The Lord's Prayer" or "The Lord is my Shepherd". If RC, finish by a blessing with Holy Water.
9. *Finish up-* with a hug if this is appropriate and allowed.

More alternative activities during the visit.

If religious or otherwise interested, take for a visit to the Chapel (if available).

If musical, play some of their favourite CDs, especially if they belonged to a choir. Most musical items can also be found on the visitor's YouTube.

If the resident is in a wheelchair, possibly take around the grounds for a short time, or to visit other residents they know (if this is allowed).

Visiting people coming towards the end of their lives

These tips are based on my limited experience with seven people in nursing homes as they reached the end of their lives. I had visited them regularly over a number of years so that we were familiar with each other, and I was reasonably well-versed in what was meaningful to them. The following key words reflect what I found helpful.

1. Presence
2. Tenderness
3. Time
4. Familiarity
5. Touch (provisional)
6. Prayer that is familiar, or a hymn, a Psalm or Scripture reading

1. *Presence*: No matter how tired the person is, a quiet presence is generally appreciated, without any demands being made on the one being visited.
2. *Tenderness*: This is shown by a smile and a gentle, caring tone of voice, offering comfort with no expectation of conversation.
3. *Time*: The visit needs to be unhurried and relaxed. The visitor listens and responds to whatever the resident wants to talk about, especially if this is emotional in content, e.g. gratitude or disquiet.
4. *Familiarity*: To the extent that the visitor knows the person being visited, comforting memories can be triggered regarding family, happy times etc. If the person being visited has dementia, routines already established can recall familiar material, including prayers, poems, hymns, songs etc.
5. *Touch*: Provided social distance is not required. If it is required, then touch has to be omitted; otherwise, squeezing or shaking a hand, a hug, holding a hand, an arm around the person's shoulder, etc., reduces loneliness and gives the feeling of human warmth.
6. *Prayer*: This could be a prayer that is familiar to the person; "The Lord's my Shepherd" (Psalm 22/23) is familiar to all Christian denominations (for RCs, see p.50 and the prayer below.)

"Jesus, Mary and Joseph, I give you my heart and my soul,
Jesus, Mary and Joseph, assist me now and in my last moments.
Jesus, Mary and Joseph, may I breathe forth my soul
in peace with you. Amen"

Another shortened prayer could be part of the Hail Mary, as follows

"Holy Mary, Mother of God, pray for us sinners, now and at
the hour of our death. Amen."

or (if more appropriate)

"Holy Mary, Mother of God, pray for me now at
the hour of my death, Amen."

Ask the person you are visiting if they would like you to pray with them. If the answer is yes, ask if they have a particular prayer. Most times, the person has a favourite prayer. Then add others as appropriate (examples suggested above and in a later section of this booklet, p.49)

Other advice

From reviewing notes that I have made over the years, the following observations may be of help:

- What the person most wants is to feel at peace.
- They need to love and be loved and to be ready to let go.
- Make sure that others looking after them realise the importance of "attending to small things that matter to them".

- Their preferences and choices should be respected.
- It is important not to talk about them in their presence but to talk to them as appropriate.
- Privacy is needed at this time, as is quietness in the area where they are.
- In the process of dying, the person needs warm human contact.
- It would be good for the person to be able to hold a personal item of deep sentimental value or a religious item such as a crucifix, a rosary, a prayer book etc.

Trained Chaplains:

In addition, trained chaplains could explore other more personal avenues that would not usually be appropriate for non-trained visitors, including:

- Helping them to articulate how they are emotionally.
- Getting them to look back on life and its meaning, including suffering.
- Understanding their anxiety, their need for reassurance, and unresolved feelings of grief, anger, loss, also self-blame.
- Asking, 'what particular things are on your mind right now?'

These kinds of questions, while they might be suggestions or guides, probably should not be broached until there is some relationship of trust between the visitor and the person. This relationship, in some cases, can be established quickly, and in others, it takes time. It is essential that the person doesn't feel intruded upon.

These are a couple of tips that might help to put the person at ease and help the visitor to get to know the person:
- Notice what's in the person's environment – pictures, books, beads, wedding ring etc. "The flowers, the football match and the pictures are the small change of human relationships" (origin unknown).
- A question such as "What's the hardest part?" can often be an opener for the person to talk.

- Sometimes, when appropriate, ask the person if they would like a blessing or the sacrament of the sick.
- Remember, when visiting someone who is actively dying, there may be family or friends present; these can be ministered to also, and it is important to include them.
- Most importantly, the visitor should be themselves. Patients can sense if the visitor is trying too hard. The patient is the most important person in this relationship.

It is important to avoid bringing the person down a road on which one may be unable to offer support. Know when to seek specialist advice, if appropriate, and with the person's permission.

Finally, remember to prepare yourself psychologically for the visit, and if you are a religious person, pray for the person yourself and pray for guidance.

Reading Reference

A Practical Guide to the Spiritual Care of the Dying Person (written by a working group for the Catholic Bishops of England and Wales.) (2010) Published by Catholic Truth Society (CTS) and available through Veritas Publications, Lower Abbey St. Dublin 1.

Visiting when there are restrictions in place such as in time of pandemic

Considering the problems involved for the visitor and the person being visited, it would seem true to say that the main problem is communication. Apart from the communication between visitor and resident, essential matters such as policy, practice and personal application of restrictions need to be shared between the resident and nursing home management as well as between the visitor and the nursing home. This is also true for the stage when restrictions are being eased. Protecting everybody from infection is paramount, so Public Health Guidelines must be followed. Visits may need to be pre-booked. On arrival, the routine may include temperature being taken, hands sanitised, masks being worn, and contact details taken as the visitor is signed in. When restrictions are easing, the use of human connection, touch etc., should be cleared with staff before being reintroduced.

The challenge facing the visitor is to try to understand the nature of the communication problems that can be involved.

What you need to know about communication and how it works:

1. Why and how we communicate (see p.8 of this booklet and further information below)
2. The changes to the older person's communication due to ageing and acquired neurological conditions. (see obstacles to communication below)
3. How to facilitate interaction and accommodate these changes, such as increasing clarity (see verbal communication below)
4. The need for engagement - giving time and attention to the current interaction

When might you need this knowledge?
- When preparing for the visit during restricted visiting, such as window visits, the visitor will bring items of interest to the resident, e.g. photographs or pictures and other paraphernalia.
- During the visit, when these props can be helpful to maintain the resident's attention.
- After the visit, when the person's preferences can be noted for future reference, also what they responded to during the visit.

Why is it important to be informed?
- To have a more rewarding visit.
- To communicate respectfully.
- To take into consideration the needs of the resident, visitor and staff.

How do we communicate?

Verbal Communication:
We talk using vocabulary and language. The more specific the vocabulary, the better we can make ourselves understood. If a message needs to be relayed, it should be very clear. Short, succinct sentences can be of more value, heard and understood more easily.

Nonverbal Communication:
This includes body language (gestures, posture etc.), facial expression (smiling, laughing, looking cross or angry etc.) and tone of voice (soothing, angry, humorous and loudness or softness).

When wearing a mask, slightly exaggerated movements and facial expressions can be helpful and, in some cases, essential. Examples of these are nodding or shaking the head, 'thumbs up', lifting shoulders or a hand on the heart for sympathy.

Listening and understanding:
Conversations involve listening and turn-taking. Making deliberate eye contact with the older person before we speak alerts them to pay attention to us. After we speak, pausing and waiting will allow time for the older person to formulate a response. Allowing them to speak without interruption and reflecting back what they have told us shows that we are listening.

Obstacles to Communication during a Pandemic:

The older person may already have difficulty understanding the words and sentences spoken to them, remembering words, putting words together into sentences or taking turns in a conversation.

They may have a hearing loss and need support and encouragement to wear their hearing aid during or before a visit so that conversations are more successful.

Infection control measures such as face masks and social distancing add to any existing challenges to communication.

The H.S.E has approved a selection of transparent masks (as distinct from visors); when worn by the visitor, they allow the older person to notice facial expressions more easily and observe the visitor's mouth as they speak.

We can communicate our positive regard/ love for the person being visited, despite any obstacles, by simply being present.

We can facilitate interaction by sharing meaningful visual props such as photographs and other items that reflect the person's interests.

We can support conversational turn-taking by commenting on each item we share without asking direct questions or expecting a verbal response. The older person may reply with a few words or respond non-verbally by smiling or pointing; this can be our cue to take another turn in the conversation by smiling and making another short comment.

Courtesy and Common Sense:

Many nursing homes have difficulty due to a shortage of available staff during a pandemic, especially at weekends. Understandably, this can lead to related problems for both the resident and family members. Also, if agency staff are employed, they may not be as familiar with individual residents as regular staff.

Not every problem associated with a pandemic can be solved by being given a list of tips. It is essential to use courtesy and common sense, inform ourselves as far as possible, and share our successes with those interested.

Technology can play a part as an aide to communication during restrictions:

Mobile Phones:

In some situations, such as 'window visits', it has been helpful for both visitors and residents to use a mobile phone so that sound can be amplified and they can hear and be heard.

Tablet or iPad:

For many residents, a Tablet or iPad has given them great comfort by letting them see and speak to family members who cannot visit. In addition to acquiring the Tablet, some preparation for a session on a Tablet will be necessary and will require the cooperation of staff.

In many cases, **Activity Organisers** are the people who plan and look after these virtual visits. The following section comes from one such Activity Organiser – Sarah Cairns, from Bantry Community Hospital in Co.Cork - who obliged with the following helpful tips and contributed her observations which are included in this section.

Tips for a virtual visit

Using a Tablet or iPad:

✓ Having a regular slot, as well as a positive routine for the person/ resident, is helpful. Staff may prepare for your call by:
  - Having the tablet charged and connected to the wifi.
  - Bringing the person to their room or a quiet space to receive the call.
  - Setting up a table with a non-stick mat underneath the tablet and a solid/heavy implement that the tablet can lean against that will keep the tablet focused on the person's face, hands-free.
  - Ensuring the volume is adequate for the person, speakers may be required.

✓ Remind the care centre/nursing home on the morning of the visit of the time that you will call at, and the medium that you will use ie: *Face Book Messenger- face calling / Zoom / Facetime / Skype or WhatsApp video call.*
This is advised before each call as different staff members work different days and all staff are not familiar with all of the above mediums.

✓ Call at the agreed time as staff can have other things to do and may be waiting for your call.

✓ Make sure that your image is in the middle of the screen, so the person can see you correctly (otherwise, it may be that many conversations are had while a person's eyes only are peeping up at the bottom of the screen.) You might judge this by ensuring there is no gap between the top of your head and the top of your image. It is essential that the person can see the caller correctly for recognition, interpreting body language, lip reading and eye contact.

✓ Before the staff member/care partner leaves, ensure that the person can hear you clearly; the volume may need to be adjusted.

✓ If appropriate, a parcel could be sent in anticipation of the call containing some of the items mentioned above, e,g. a small item, verse or prayer, pictures of the local area to discuss etc.

✓ Offer to call the care centre/nursing home when the call has ended to alert staff that it has ended.

✓ NOTE: *The situation changes several times during the course of the pandemic, so you need to be alert to the current regulations or easing of restrictions from time to time.*

With thanks to Sarah Cairns, Activity Coordinator, Bantry General Hospital

❧ PART 2 ❧

Spirituality and Religious Practices

66
One of the many definitions of spirituality is 'that which gives continuing meaning and purpose to a person's life and nourishes their inner being.'

Albert Jewell "Ageing, Spirituality and Well-being" 2004

Broadly speaking, spirituality is about relationships with God (or a Higher Being), oneself, others, and nature.

Relationship with God is addressed through ritual, prayer and faith sharing; with oneself, through self-knowledge, forgiveness, care of health (physical and mental) and having a sense of humour; with others, through communication, good relationships, shared interests and celebration; with nature, through access to beauty, gardens and gardening, scenery, visual art – painting, art appreciation, music and song, including birdsong and poetry depicting nature.

In the words of the poet Brendan Kennelly, 'Self knows that self is not enough'.

Much research has gone into identifying spiritual needs in older people. One study focussed on the perceived needs of a large group of older people living in a care situation. They identified the following as spiritual needs:

- Religious beliefs and practices
- Absolution
- Connectedness
- Comfort and reassurance
- Healing
- Searching for meaning and purpose

Spiritual Reading

This could be a personal choice of reading Scripture from any part of the Bible on a regular basis or '**Lectio Divina**' (A Latin expression which means sacred reading) This is done in three stages

1. **Reading:** you read the passage slowly and reverentially, allowing the words to sink into your consciousness.
2. **Meditation:** you allow the passage to stir up memories within you so that you recognise in it your own experience or that of people who have touched your life.
3. **Prayer:** you allow the meditation to lead you to prayer- thanksgiving, humility and petition.

> ❝
> **Bible reading is a personal encounter with God,
> a communion which resembles (though different from)
> the communion of the Eucharist.**
>
> *Fr.Michel De Verteuil C.S.Sp.*

(NOTE: It dates back to the time of St. Benedict 400/500 AD)
The basic principle of 'Lectio Divina' is that Bible reading is a personal encounter with God. We love the text, linger over it, read it over and over and let it remain with us. It stirs feelings; we identify with the characters; we feel for them, admire them or dislike them.

Gradually we 'recognise' the text; we find that we have lived the sequence of events ourselves or have seen them lived in others who have touched our lives for good or ill.

Alternatively, spiritual reading could focus on particular authors and their publications, or religious magazines might be the choice for those with a short attention span. For older people who can manage technology, YouTube offers extensive material for reflection, e.g. *Daniel O'Leary, Ronald Rolheiser, Robert Barron, Richard Rohr* and more.

Also, actor *Alex McCowen* reads the entire Gospel of St. Mark, lasting 1hr 44 mins. *David Suchet* has recorded the complete Bible. Both of these are also available on YouTube.

The Present Moment

A feeling of calm is a great help when wanting to give one's full attention to prayer and the presence of God.

Many people find distractions get in the way of focussing on prayer, so here is a practice that might help. In a popular sense, this could be referred to as mindfulness or Christian Meditation, but it could also be called: *Relax, focus, and experience living peacefully in the present moment.'*

To do this, it is necessary to focus on gathering your thoughts, which otherwise risk tiring out your brain. While aiming to use your breath as the focus, begin the exercise by checking yourself out as follows

1. What thoughts are going on in your head? Name them and then let them go.
2. What feelings are there? Just name them. Then let them go -don't judge them.
3. What body sensations are there? Are your shoulders tense? Drop them and relax that area of your body.
4. Next, move to your breath. Say 'IN' as you breathe in; say 'OUT' as you breathe out.
5. Then say 'Breathing in – ONE; breathing out - ONE'.
6. 'Breathing in - TWO; breathing out - TWO'.
7. Continue up to FIVE and start from ONE again.
8. Return to your body and your facial expression. Are you relaxed or not? Loosen up your muscles and your posture. Relax and accept just how you are and how you feel without judging.

NOTE: This is based on an exercise called "Three Minute Breathing Space" in a book by Mark Williams called "Mindfulness – Finding Peace in a Frantic World " recommended by Tony Bates, a Psychologist who wrote a weekly column on mindfulness in the Irish Times in 2013,

You can add a spiritual dimension to this exercise by substituting appropriate words, for those in the example above, e.g. *'Peace IN', 'Anxiety or anger / sadness / disquiet etc OUT'* or other suitable alternatives, e.g. *'Let go of thought and simply be (or let Love be)'.*

A Spirituality based on the Present Moment:

Surrendering to God's will requires living in and acknowledging the sacrament of the present moment, a phrase most famously used in the 17th century by Fr. Jeanne-Pierre de Caussade S.J. in his classic book 'Abandonment to Divine Providence'.

This phrase means we need to lovingly accept whatever God is allowing, in His divine will, at each moment, being wholly indifferent to what I may perceive as "bad" things in life, such as something not going my way or a suffering I wish I did not have to endure.

In this spirituality, we live each moment confidently as a blessing from God, full of faith and gratitude for His love and mercy – not anxious about the future, bogged down by the past, but surrendering each moment to the One who is love.

Spiritual Reminiscence

"Spiritual Reminiscence is a way of communicating that acknowledges the person as a spiritual being and seeks to engage the person in a more meaningful and personal way." McKinlay and Trevitt 2015.
It can be done individually or in a group and takes place as a conversation between the speaker(s) and the listener.

It covers the individual's life story by reminiscing about the past and the feelings that these memories evoke, and by reflecting on the present and how they feel about things, people and circumstances that challenge them.

When painful memories or observations feature, the purpose is to help the person re-frame these memories by considering them objectively. With the passage of time, they begin to grow into a new understanding of experiences that have negatively affected them.

It is a way of helping the person you are talking with identify what is most meaningful to them right now, what is most important, what is hardest for them and what gives them joy and keeps them going.

Always encourage the person to share a bit more without any pressure. For example, after a pause, simply repeat their last few words or a significant phrase they have just used. Allow for silence and give time to listening. Emphasise confidentiality.

What were the best relationships in their lives? Do they have friends now? What are their worries and fears? What do they think God is like? What are their early memories of praying? Who gives them spiritual support now? A series of questions can be spaced out over a period of six weekly meetings.

The Practice of Spiritual Reminiscence:

As with all conversations that go well, there needs to be a relaxed atmosphere, a positive relationship between participants and the ability to express feelings in suitable words while the facilitator listens. Begin by suggesting that we will look back at life as well as life as it is now. Pose one of a number of definite questions, e.g. over the six weeks, the topics suggested are:

1. Life meaning
2. Relationships and connecting
3. Hopes, fears and worries
4. Growing older and transcendence
5. Spiritual beliefs
6. Spiritual practices

Religious Practices:

1. Prayer: the primary purpose of which is to grow in a personal relationship with God, although prayer is often focused on particular intentions such as praying for someone's good health, exam results, safety etc.
2. Group attendance at Mass or religious service, Rosary, the sacraments, Eucharist, Reconciliation, the sacrament of the sick (anointing).
3. Personal practices include being connected to live-streamed services or Masses.
4. Individual conversation with visiting chaplain, ordained or non-ordained or pastoral carer.
5. Personal recitation of the Rosary or Divine Office, or even a shorter form of these two – one decade of the Rosary or one Psalm, or just holding a Rosary Beads in their hands.
6. Familiar prayers, including Ciúnas CDs of favourite hymns and prayers for RCs, available from 'Engaging Dementia' (01 2608138)

The following is an example of the kind of prayer that many people find particularly meaningful, regardless of age.

"Lord, I trust in you in whom I believe. You have your reasons for everything.
Your measure of work is not ours, your plans are not ours but yours are best, better than ours.
You bring forth fruit as you please when you please and in the way you please.
It is enough that I wait doing what I can. I desire to belong to you.
Let the rest be as you wish."

Archbishop Goodier SJ

Spiritual Companionship

Once an individual is enthusiastic about living more reflectively and sharing their lives spiritually, a schedule for visiting can be agreed upon. As for the frequency of visits, these could be fortnightly and last an average of 45 minutes. It would then be possible to see two residents in turn for Nursing Home visits. It could form part of a more extended visit for a person living at home.

Some of those being visited may believe that as they grow older, they are being drawn to a closer relationship with God. They value any opportunity to pursue a spiritual life that meets these deeper spiritual needs.

Spiritual Companionship grows out of a relationship of trust between the resident and visitor. It is for people of faith who may have started by being visited as part of Companionship visiting. In getting to know a person, it becomes possible to gauge their interest in living at a deeper level.

The visits are not like Spiritual Direction and Spiritual Reminiscence; they are distinct in that they involve the resident and visitor sharing spiritually. The aim is to allow for continuing growth in relationship with God while coming to terms with the challenges of life, especially later life.

The main feature of the visit is 'finding God in all things', through
- Praying with scripture through the practice of 'Lectio Divina', which can focus on the following Sunday's gospel or any passage that has a spiritual appeal for them.
- Finding God in real life as it presents itself day by day in the things, people and circumstances that challenge us.

It includes silence and voluntary sharing in conversation.

Finding God in Scripture:

This could be the prayerful reading of the Bible, using a passage of choice, following the liturgical year by reading prayerfully the scriptures allocated to a particular day or by using the Lectio Divina approach as explained in p.40.

Lectio Divina, a Latin expression that means sacred reading, is a way of praying with scripture that shows us that gospel stories are life-giving when we connect them with our own story and our experience of the world at large. As we reflect, we see how the passage touches us and stirs concrete memories (not insights)

- In our emotions – how do you feel about it?
- In our intellect – what do you think about it?
- In our experience – what memories does it evoke?

We bring these memories to God in prayer.

Finding God in Everyday Life:

The following extracts are taken from "The Joy of God", the collected writings of Sr. Mary David OSB 2019, available from The Tablet Bookshop, through Bloomsbury Continuum publishers or from Veritas. The first extract is from a chapter on spiritual growth in which she advises:

> 66 *There's no need to be at war about everything. Try receiving things as a gift, try to enjoy and give a positive interpretation to whatever you might be feeling resistance to. Believe me; you will become a different person. Go towards whatever is coming, announced; it is coming from God. Go along with things, people, circumstances. It's your resistance that is causing you so much distress and pain and not the issues themselves.*
>
> *Trust that whatever we give over to God, he will transform, he will make what is good even more so, and whatever is harmful, he will heal ... Keep on trying to be faithful to the present moment, accepting what it brings.*

The second is from a chapter on Freedom (another word for 'choice')

> *It is our choice to be miserable or agitated or else to ignore it all. We are not made or unmade by what happens on the outside but by our response to it.*
>
> *We are responsible for how other people affect us. The other person is not responsible for how they affect us. It is your choice if you allow others to affect you just because they are upset about something (especially when it has nothing to do with you). You have a choice. You can choose not to be affected by them. In a sense, when you get low over other people's moods or whatever, you have 'given them permission' to affect you in this way. It is not a question of temperament. It is a question of choice.*

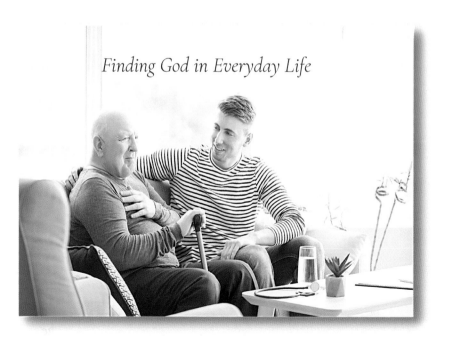

Finding God in Everyday Life

The following reflection and prayer reflect the spirituality contained in the above book.

'My soul is longing for your peace, near to you, my God.'
Peace is attained by growing in loving compliance with
the will of God and finding God in all things.
The Fundamental fact is that God loves me.
I can tell him that I love him too, but he said repeatedly, 'If
you love me, you will keep my commandments', i.e. I will do
his will. His will is to be found in the nitty-gritty of everyday
things that I either welcome and embrace or that I resist and
don't accept and go along with. These include things, people
and circumstances that come my way each day.'

'Heavenly Father, giver of hope, I begin a new day confident
that you come to me in all circumstances and make all things
work for the fulfilment of your purposes'

(Companion to the Breviary)

PRAYER

Help me, Lord, to go along with the things, people and circumstances
that will come my way today, those that I welcome and embrace and
others and that I am tempted to resist and fight against.
Help me to trust in Divine Providence and to grow in loving
compliance with your will as the best expression of my love for you.

Thank you, God, for ALL THAT IS

Selected Prayers

The following selection of prayers are a resource to fall back on:

Dear Jesus, make yourself to me a living bright reality
More present to faith's vision keen than any outward
object seen, More dear, more intimately nigh than e'en
the sweetest human tie.
(*said to be the favourite prayer of Edel Quinn, Legionary*).

When needing Divine Assistance to cope with everyday challenges:

'Heavenly Father, giver of hope, I begin a new day confident that you
come to me in all things, people and circumstances and make all
things work for the fulfilment of your purposes'. Help me to go along
with things, people and circumstances, to accept and stop resisting
the challenges they present to me, to trust in Divine Providence and
to grow in loving compliance with your will as the best expression of
my love for you. Amen'
(*Adapted from People's Companion to the Breviary*)

A form of silent prayer, enjoying God's presence:

Let Your God Love you.
Be silent, be still.
Alone, empty before your God.
Say nothing, ask nothing.
Be silent, be still.
Let your God look upon you.
That is all, He knows.
He understands, He loves you with
an enormous love.
He only wants to look upon you
with His Love.
Quiet, Still be.
Let your God – love you.
(*Composed by Edwina Gateley*)

When asking for the presence of God to touch those you meet:

Dear Jesus, help me to spread your fragrance everywhere I
go; flood my soul with your spirit and life, penetrate and
possess my whole being so utterly that every soul I come in
contact with may feel your presence in my soul; let them
look up and see no longer me but only Jesus.
(Prayer of Cardinal Newman)

The prayer of Archbishop Goodier S.J. already included in 'Religious
Practices (see p.45) can be used at any time. It is an everyday prayer.

Traditional Catholic Prayers

*While these prayers may not be familiar to the visitor, they may be
important to and bring comfort to the resident.*

The Lord's Prayer

In the name of the Father, and of the Son,
and of the Holy Spirit. Amen.
Our Father,
who art in heaven,
hallowed be thy name;
thy kingdom come;
thy will be done
on earth as it is in heaven.
Give us this day our daily bread,
and forgive us our trespasses
as we forgive those who trespass against us,
and lead us not into temptation,
but deliver us from evil.
Amen.

The Hail Mary

Hail Mary, full of grace,
the Lord is with thee.
Blessed are you among women,
and blessed is the fruit of thy womb, Jesus.
Holy Mary, Mother of God,
pray for us sinners,
now and at the hour of our death.
Amen.

The Gloria Patri

Glory be to the Father, and to the Son,
and to the Holy Spirit.
As it was in the beginning,
is now, and ever shall be,
world without end.
Amen.

Guardian Angel Prayer

O angel of God, my guardian dear,
to whom God's love commits me here,
ever this day be at my side,
to light and guard, to rule and guide.
Amen.

Memorare

Remember, O most gracious Virgin Mary,
that never was it known
that anyone who fled to your protection,
implored your help or sought your intercession was left unaided.
Inspired by this confidence,
I fly unto thee O virgin of virgins my mother.
To thee I come, before thee I am sinful and sorrowful.
O Mother of the Word Incarnate,
despise not my petitions but in thy clemency, hear and answer them.
Amen.

Hail, Holy Queen

Hail, holy Queen, Mother of mercy,
Hail, our life, our sweetness, and our hope.
To thee do we cry, poor banished children of Eve;
To thee do we send up our sighs,
Mourning and weeping in this valley of tears
O mother of the word Incarnate Despise not our petitions but in thy
clemency, hear and answer them. Amen
O clement, O loving, O sweet Virgin Mary. Pray for us O Holy Mother
God, that we may be made worthy of the promises of Christ.

The Prayer to Saint Michael the Archangel

Blessed Michael the Archangel, defend us in in the day of conflict.
Be our safeguard against the wickedness and snares of the devil; May
God rebuke him, we humbly pray; And do thou, O Prince of the
Heavenly Host, by the power of God, thrust Satan into hell and all
evil spirits who wander through the world for the ruin of souls.
Amen.

The Angelus

The angel of the Lord declared unto Mary,
And she conceived of the Holy Spirit
Hail Mary, full of grace ....
Behold the handmaid of the Lord,
Be it done unto me according to your word
Hail Mary...
And the Word was made flesh,
And dwelt among us.
Hail Mary...
Pray for us, O Holy Mother Of God,
That we may be made worthy of the promised of Christ.
Let Us Pray
Pour forth we beseech thee O Lord, thy grace into our hearts, that we
to whom the incarnation of Christ thy Son was made known by the
message of an angel, may by his passion and cross be brought to the
resurrection, through Christ our Lord. Amen.

⁓⅋ Acknowledgements ⅋⁓

I wish to express sincere gratitude to Dr Noel Keating for his careful reading of the script and the many suggestions he made, which added to the clarity and accuracy of the content. He also advised on a plan to make the booklet available to as many potential visitors as possible.

Edel, a former speech and language therapy colleague, generously offered to format the script for printing. Her knowledge of technology, including graphics, has added much to the final version of the booklet.

Sarah Cairns, an Activities Coordinator attached to Bantry General Hospital, contributed to the section on visiting during a pandemic. She shared her experience of using technology to help bridge the communication gap when personal visits were severely restricted.

Carmel Molloy, a former hospital chaplain, shared her experience of visiting when the person being visited was approaching the end of life.

At the earlier stage of this project, when a draft was sent out to a small number of those interested, I received valuable suggestions which have been incorporated into this final text of the booklet. I am very grateful to all who replied and contributed, namely, Lucy, Bernadette, Carmel, Eibhlis and Donal.

Finally, I would like to acknowledge the ongoing practical help given to me by the Religious Sisters of Charity, who have made the production of this booklet possible.

❧ About the Author ❧

Mary Threadgold was born in Dublin and joined the Religious Sisters of Charity in the 1950s. After her Profession as a Religious Sister of Charity, she qualified as a Speech and Language Therapist in London, later doing an MSc in Human Communication at the University of London.

Mary worked with a wide variety of people with communication disorders until she moved to Ballybane, Galway, in the 1980s, where she specialised in Intellectual Disabilities. In the absence of meaningful language, she noticed the positive effect of music and touch as a facilitator of communication.

She had often been struck by the sight of older people in nursing homes, gathered together in day rooms without interacting or being communicated with, many of whom were living with dementia. Influenced by her training and her conviction that love and respect needed to underpin any professional approach to meeting the communication needs of such a group of older people, she turned her attention to them.

Her background as a Sister of Charity also influenced her desire to make a difference to the lives of this group, many of whom were living with dementia. Additionally, having grown up with grandparents with whom she was very close, Mary felt an affinity with older people. She believed that many nursing home residents had been seen by a Speech and Language Therapist but that therapy may have been discontinued, as at that time, it was no longer deemed to be effective.

Finally, in 1990, Mary decided to design a therapeutic intervention for this group. Drawing on her expertise and experience, the activity was based on sensory engagement, structure and repetition, with an emphasis on communication and quality interaction. She named the activity Sonas, the Irish word for joy and contentment. She added the abbreviation 'aPc', meaning activating Potential for communication, to underline the rationale for this approach.

With the support of the Religious Sisters of Charity and later the Irish Department of Health, Mary produced the programme materials and began training healthcare staff to implement the programme. Sonas aPc was established as a not for profit organisation in 1996.

In 2005 Mary's interest in dementia took on a new meaning when her brother, her only sibling, developed Lewy Body disease. She visited him three times a week in his nursing home for seven years.

Since her retirement in 2016 from Sonas aPc, now called 'Engaging Dementia', Mary has focused her attention on spiritual care and befriending. She drafted the materials for a befriending toolkit that Engaging Dementia is now producing. She recently developed a guide promoting companionship for visitors to enhance their relationship with older people in long-stay care.